FAITH
unfolded

A FRESH LOOK AT
THE REFORMED FAITH

JIM OSTERHOUSE

**FAITH
ALIVE.**
Christian Resources

Grand Rapids, Michigan

Cover photo: Janis Christie / © PhotoDisc

Quotations from *Grace Unknown* by R. C. Sproul, © 1997, used by permission of Baker Book House Company.

Unless otherwise indicated, the Scripture quotations in this publication are from the HOLY BIBLE, NEW INTERNATIONAL VERSION, © 1973, 1978, 1984, International Bible Society. Used by permission of Zondervan Bible Publishers.

We welcome your comments. Call 1-800-333-8300 or e-mail us at editors@faithaliveresources.org.

ISBN 1-56212-554-0

10 9 8 7 6 5 4 3

Contents

Foreword

This booklet arises directly out of the mission of the church. As a church planter I would always include a discussion of the "doctrines of grace" as a part of any new member class. I used the common acrostic T.U.L.I.P. to teach these truths, but found that it created more confusion than clarity.

For years I made this offer—"A free steak dinner for anyone who can come up with a better acrostic." One day Rod Marks, a school teacher and baseball coach who was only two months old in the faith (Rod has since gone to his eternal reward), came into my office, handed me a piece of paper, and said: "Here is your acrostic." It was F.A.I.T.H. (Rod would not accept the steak dinner, but did finally bring his family over to our house for steaks on the grill.)

Since then I have taught these wonderful truths using F.A.I.T.H., polishing and improving the concepts over the years. Whenever I would share F.A.I.T.H. with other pastors and church planters they would say, "You ought to write that up!" So here it is.

May it be a great aid to you as you build God's church and kingdom by seeking the lost and discipling the found.

—*Jim Osterhouse*
Lombard, Illinois

Introduction

Things are not always as they appear. There is a building in Orlando, Florida, that is lying upside down on its roof. The side wall is split open where it apparently landed on top of another building. Was this the result of a tornado? A hurricane? No. The building is a tourist attraction that was intentionally constructed to grab people's attention.

The Christian faith is not what it first appears to be either. On the surface salvation seems like a cooperative effort between God and people—God provides the sacrifice of his Son Jesus to pay the price of sin, and people provide the faith to receive the gift of salvation. A closer inspection of the Bible reveals something quite different. This booklet will explain the true nature of faith by unfolding five biblical facts.

These teachings are sometimes referred to as "the five points of Calvinism," but that is really a misnomer. John Calvin did not invent these teachings. They are clearly found on the pages of Holy Scripture.

A better name for these teachings is the "doctrines of grace," for they systematically explain the true meaning of grace—that is, what the Bible really teaches about sin and salvation. We will learn about these doctrines of grace using a simple memory tool, the acronym F.A.I.T.H.

A Note to Study Group Leaders

For years I have used this material in new member classes, in teaching, and with individuals. Seekers who asked about these biblical teachings were helped. Even those who had been Christians for many years have benefited from a review of the truths explained here. (The pamphlet *F.A.I.T.H. Unfolded* is an excellent abbreviated version of this material. Copies are available from CRC Publications, 1-800-333-8300.)

Here are some other suggested uses:

- Give a copy to someone who shows interest, and follow up with conversation.

- Keep a supply on hand to give to inquirers.

- Give the *F.A.I.T.H. Unfolded* pamphlet to a seeker and then follow up with the book.

- Keep a copy in your church library for reference when someone asks about the ideas explained in this book.

If you are leading a class, the material in this book can be divided into two sessions (chapters 1-6 and 7-10) or three sessions (chapters 1-5; 6-8; 9-10). Or you may choose a slower pace of one or two chapters per session.

Start by giving an overview of the material the first week that you meet. Distribute the books to group members and ask them to read the chapters you will cover in your second session. Ask them to read the discussion questions (included with each chapter) too. Group members may want to write down ideas the discussion questions bring to mind or questions of their own in the margins of their books. As much as possible, encourage group members to ask questions, to express their doubts, and to seek the reassurance that comes from a healthy, Spirit-directed discussion.

As you plan each session, allow plenty of time for group discussion. Participation is key to the success of your group. Don't be afraid of silence, and don't pressure people to speak if they are uncomfortable doing so. Asking discussion questions of your own will help to draw out the thoughts of your group members too.

As you bring the study to a close using chapter 10, be aware that some individuals in your group may have no assurance that they are among the elect of God. This may be quite troubling to them. Be sensitive to their situation and openly invite any group members who are unsure of their salvation to speak with you privately after the session. Prepare yourself beforehand for these conversations by engaging in sincere prayer and gathering relevant Scripture passages to share.

God is pleased when the basics of the Christian faith are unfolded to people who have never heard. May he bless your efforts today.

Fallen Humankind

"F" is for Fallen Humankind
"A" is for Adopted by God
"I" is for Intentional Atonement
"T" is for Transformed by the Holy Spirit
"H" is for Held by God

"F" stands for "fallen humankind." Adam, the first person who ever lived on earth, represented all of humanity when he fell into sin. The Bible says that "sin entered the world through one man" (Rom. 5:12), and that one man was Adam (Gen. 3:1-7). But when Adam fell, how far did he fall? Did he fall completely or only partially? Are people today—who are physical descendants of Adam—completely helpless in the grip of sin or can they contribute something to their salvation?

Let's look at some Scripture passages to understand what the Bible says about this. The apostle Paul writes in Romans 3:23: "For all have sinned and fall short of the glory of God."

To "fall short" of something—a goal, for example—means that we fail to reach that goal. This verse says that all people fall short of the glory of God. That means that we are completely unable to match the perfect righteousness that God requires of us. We fall short. We miss it. We may try to reach it, but we can't. We fail completely. This is far different than saying that we get partway there, or that we reach part of our goal.

To illustrate this point, imagine that we are visiting a tall skyscraper in the center of a large city. As we enter the atrium of the building, I ask you to remain on the first floor while I walk up to the mezzanine level. Then as you watch from below, I get up on the railing, jump off, and hit the floor, breaking a leg and a couple of ribs. Though injured and hurting badly, I am still able to help myself. So I drag myself to a telephone and dial 911 for help. That is how some people understand humankind's fall into sin. We have fallen into sin, they say, but we can still help ourselves toward salvation since we are only partially immobilized by our fall.

Now, let's say I am miraculously healed from my injuries. I stand up and say to you, "I will now demonstrate the Reformed understanding of the extent of our fall into sin." I ask you to go outside and stand on the sidewalk while I take the elevator to the top of the tower and make my way to the edge of the building. Again you watch in horror as I jump from 110 floors up. When I hit the pavement, I am killed. There is nothing I can do to help myself. I am completely wiped out. Only God can help me, for I am dead. That is what it means to be totally fallen into sin.

Turn in the Bible to Ephesians 2:1: "As for you, you were *dead* in your transgressions and sins, in which you used to live. . . ." That is the Reformed understanding: We are *dead* in our sins. The apostle Paul goes on to write:

> As for you, you were dead in your transgressions and sins, in which you used to live when you followed the ways of this world and of the ruler of the kingdom of the air, the spirit who is now at work in those who are disobedient. All of us also lived among them at one time, gratifying the cravings of our sinful nature and following its desires and thoughts. Like the rest, we were by nature objects of wrath. But because of his great love for us, God, who is rich in mercy, *made us alive with Christ even when we were dead in transgressions—it is by grace you have been saved.* And God raised us up with Christ and seated us with him in the heavenly realms in Christ Jesus (Eph. 2:1-6, emphasis added).

We were dead in our transgressions and sins, but God made us alive. To underscore the point, let's say that I am a teacher and you are one of my students. When you enter the classroom one day, you find me stretched out on the floor, very sick. Nevertheless, you ask me to bring you a glass of water. Although I am very ill, I manage to drag myself down the hall to the drinking fountain to get your water. It is very difficult to do, but I am able, and I return to the classroom with your water.

Now imagine that you entered the classroom, found me stretched out on the floor dead, and said to me, "Jim, go get me a glass of water!" What would happen? Nothing. I would not be able to do as you asked because I was dead. I would be completely incapable of responding to your request. Humankind's fall into sin is like that. It is so complete that it renders all people totally unable to respond to the message of salvation. That is what it means to be "dead in our transgressions and sins."

Now, this is terrible news! If the effect of sin is to make us totally unable to save ourselves, how can we possibly be saved? If we are spiritually dead, how can we be made alive? God does it! Jesus once was asked this very question by a man named Nicodemus. In reply, Jesus said to him: "You must be born again" (or "born anew" or "born from above," John 3:1-8). When we understand just how bad the bad news is, we comprehend more deeply just how good the good news is.

The Bible says that our salvation requires a work of God. A story in Acts 16 demonstrates this. Paul was preaching the good news to a group of women gathered by the river in Philippi. . . .

> One of those listening was a woman named Lydia, a dealer in purple cloth from the city of Thyatira, who was a worshiper of God. *The Lord opened her heart* to respond to Paul's message (Acts 16:14, emphasis added).

If the Lord had not opened her heart, Lydia could not have received Paul's message. God does in us what we are unable to do in ourselves. By nature our minds are darkened, but God enlightens us (2 Cor. 4:6). By nature we are spiritually blind (John 9:35-41), but God enables us to see (John 9:39). By nature we are spiritually deaf, but God opens our ears (Matt. 13:9-17). By nature we are unable to believe, but God gives us the gift of faith.

> For it is by grace you have been saved, through faith—and this not from yourselves, it is the gift of God—not by works, so that no one can boast. For we are God's workmanship, created in Christ Jesus to do good works, which God prepared in advance for us to do (Eph. 2:8-9).

Questions

1. Describe a serious fall that you have taken. What is the difference between that fall and a fall that is fatal?

2. Genesis 3 records the fall of Adam and Eve into sin, taking the entire human race down with them. This is referred to as "the fall." How serious was the fall? What was the impact of it? What effects of the fall do we see today?

3. What can a person do to overcome the effects of the fall?

4. How does this truth make you feel? Hopeless? Helpless? Angry? Bitter?

5. What problems does this truth create for you?

6. How does understanding the depth of the fall enhance your understanding of Jesus' death on the cross? Of salvation? Of grace?

Chapter 2

Adopted by God

"F" is for Fallen Humankind

"A" is for Adopted by God

"I" is for Intentional Atonement

"T" is for Transformed by the Holy Spirit

"H" is for Held by God

"A" stands for "adopted by God." Even as a human couple chooses to adopt a child and welcomes that child into their family, God our heavenly Father makes a deliberate choice to adopt certain people and welcome them as adopted children into his family.

The apostle Paul writes about this spiritual adoption in his letter to the Ephesians:

> Blessed be to the God and Father of our Lord Jesus Christ, who has blessed us in Christ with every spiritual blessing in the heavenly places, just as he chose us in Christ before the foundation of the world to be holy and blameless before him in love. He destined us for adoption as his children through Jesus Christ, according to the good pleasure of his will, to the praise of his glorious grace that he freely bestowed on us in the Beloved. In him we have redemption through his blood, the forgiveness of our trespasses, according to the riches of his

grace that he lavished on us. With all wisdom and insight he has made known to us the mystery of his will, according to his good pleasure that he set forth in Christ, as a plan for the fullness of time, to gather up all things in him, things in heaven and things on earth. In Christ we have also obtained an inheritance, having been destined according to the purpose of him who accomplishes all things according to his counsel and will, so that we, who were the first to set our hope on Christ, might live for the praise of his glory (Eph. 1:3-12, NRSV).

Notice God's activity in choosing us even before he created the world: "He chose us . . . before the foundation of the world. . . . He destined us for adoption as his children. . . ." Some people call this the doctrine of election. The biblical teaching of election appears throughout the Bible. Here are some examples:

- The Old Testament Israelites are God's chosen people. "For you are a people holy to the LORD your God. The LORD your God has chosen you out of all the peoples on the face of the earth to be his people, his treasured possession.

  "The LORD did not set his affection on you and choose you because you were more numerous than other peoples, for you were the fewest of all peoples. But it was because the LORD loved you and kept the oath he swore to your forefathers that he brought you out with a mighty hand and redeemed you from the land of slavery, from the power of Pharaoh king of Egypt" (Deut. 7:6-8).

- "Blessed is the nation whose God is the LORD, the people he chose for his inheritance" (Ps. 33:12).

- "But we ought always to thank God for you, brothers loved by the Lord, because from the beginning God chose you to be saved through the sanctifying work of the Spirit and through belief in the truth" (2 Thess. 2:13).

- "Therefore, brothers and sisters, be all the more eager to confirm your call and election" (2 Pet. 1:10, NRSV).

- Jesus says of the end times, "If those days had not been cut short, no one would survive, but for the sake of the elect those days will be shortened" (Matt. 24:22).

The Bible clearly teaches that God has elected those who will be saved. You may well ask, *"On what basis* did God elect those who are elected?" Did God elect them before they had faith or because they had faith? The Bible says that although the elect were dead in their sins—and therefore incapable of exercising faith—God chose to adopt them through Christ into his family.

Jesus deals with election in John 6. Here he comments on the fact that not everyone who saw him believed in him. Why is that the case? Listen:

> Then Jesus declared, "I am the bread of life. He who comes to me will never go hungry, and he who believes in me will never be thirsty. But as I told you, you have seen me and still you do not believe. All that the Father gives me will come to me, and whoever comes to me I will never drive away. For I have come down from heaven not to do my will but to do the will of him who sent me. And this is the will of him who sent me, that I shall lose none of all that he has given me, but raise them up at the last day. For my Father's will is that everyone who looks to the Son and believes in him shall have eternal life, and I will raise him up at the last day" (John 6:35-40).

It is certainly true that "everyone who looks to the Son and believes in him shall have eternal life. . . ." But who is able to look to the Son and believe in him if all people are completely dead in their trespasses and sins? "All that the Father gives" to Jesus.

Another passage that teaches about God's choosing or electing is Acts 13. Here the apostle Paul had been preaching to the Jewish people, and they were rejecting his message. So Paul says in effect, "OK, so much for you. I am going to preach the message of salvation to the Gentiles now." Verse 48 records the Gentiles' reaction: "And when the Gentiles heard this, they were glad and honored the word of the Lord; and all who were appointed for eternal life believed." Who believed? Those who were appointed for eternal life.

Finally, we must remember that when we are elected, we are chosen for a purpose. Ephesians 2:10 says, "For we are God's workmanship, created in Christ Jesus to do good works, which God prepared in advance for us to do." We are not adopted by God so we can sit back and say, "Oh, isn't it wonderful that I am one of God's chosen people?" This was a mistake of the Old Testament Israelites. They were often proud to be God's chosen people. They gloated, saying in effect, "We are God's people. Sorry about the rest of you." God wanted them to be such a shining example to the nations that others would be attracted to them and ultimately to the living and true God. But they failed completely.

In the same way, some people misunderstand the biblical teaching of election. They see it as an issue of pride—"Oh, you think you are God's chosen people. You think you are better than us." No, not better. Those who are adopted by God realize how dead they were in their sins and how totally dependent on God they are for salvation. No, not better—the redeemed are thankful. Not better—the chosen are called to let others know the way of salvation.

In summary, Christians are adopted by God. On what basis? They are chosen, not because of good works or faith, but entirely as a result of God's love and mercy. To put it another way, God selects people as his children in Christ not because of any conditions they have met, but solely because of God's sovereign choice. This is what the Bible teaches.

Questions

1. Have you been adopted, or do you know someone who has been adopted? Have you adopted a child? How does it feel to adopt a child? To be adopted?

2. What is the process of adoption? Does the child choose his or her parents or vice versa?

3. What are some good motives for adoption?

4. Why do you think God wants to bring us into his family?

5. What can we do to make sure God selects us?

Chapter 3

Intentional Atonement

"F" is for Fallen Humankind

"A" is for Adoption by God

"I" is for Intentional Atonement

"T" is for Transformed by the Holy Spirit

"H" is for Held by God

"I" stands for "intentional atonement." Jesus died intentionally. Jesus died on the cross to save his people from their sins (Matt. 1:21). He died for those whom the Father had given him.

What we are talking about here is "atonement accomplished." Jesus died as God's appointed sacrifice for sin nearly two thousand years ago. What does that mean for us today? He accomplished the atonement on the cross. Atonement means to make satisfaction or reparation for a wrong, or to make payment. Some people divide the word this way: "at-one-ment," intending to say that we become "at one" with God once again. That is not quite right, for it describes reconciliation with God, not atonement. Reconciliation with God must be preceded by the act of atonement or payment for our sins. And that is exactly what Jesus did on the cross.

The Bible teaches that Jesus' death—his atoning work on the cross—was intentional. The apostle John quotes Jesus:

"All that the Father gives me will come to me, and whoever comes to me I will never drive away. For I have come down from heaven not to do my will but to do the will of him who sent me. And this is the will of him who sent me, that I shall lose none of all that he has given me, but raise them up at the last day. For my Father's will is that everyone who looks to the Son and believes in him shall have eternal life, and I will raise him up at the last day" (John 6:37-40).

For whom did Jesus die? He died for the ones God had given him. Anyone whom God gives to Jesus will come to Jesus and receive eternal life.

In John 10 Jesus calls himself the Good Shepherd:

"I am the good shepherd; I know my sheep and my sheep know me—just as the Father knows me and I know the Father—and I lay down my life for the sheep" (John 10:14-15).

For whom does Jesus lay down his life? For everyone? No, he lays down his life *for the sheep that the Father has given him*. Jesus continues:

"I have other sheep that are not of this sheep pen. I must bring them also. They too will listen to my voice, and there shall be one flock and one shepherd" (John 10:16).

Who are these other sheep? The initial sheep of God (people of God) were the Israelites, the Jewish people. Jesus is speaking to them and saying that he has other sheep. The Jews divided all people into two groups—Jews and non-Jews (Gentiles). Jesus says that Gentiles, too, will believe in him and be brought into the sheepfold and there will be one flock and one shepherd. Recall from chapter 2 that the Jews had misunderstood their election. They felt that they were God's chosen people and all others were not. Jesus tells them that they are wrong. Jews and Gentiles, all people, are among his sheep:

"The reason my Father loves me is that I lay down my life— only to take it up again. No one takes it from me, but I lay it down of my own accord. I have authority to lay it down and authority to take it up again. This command I received from my Father" (John 10:17-18).

Jesus' atonement on the cross was intentional. He shed his blood on purpose. The purpose was to provide atonement for all his sheep out of all peoples of the earth, both Jew and Gentile.

The intentionality of Jesus' atonement is evident not only in his death for his sheep, but also in his prayers for his sheep. His high-priestly prayer is recorded in John 17:

> "Father, . . . you granted [your Son] authority over all people that he might give eternal life to all those you have given him. . . . I have revealed you to those whom you gave me out of the world. They were yours; you gave them to me and they have obeyed your word. . . . I pray for them. I am not praying for the world, but for those you have given me, for they are yours" (John 17:1-2, 6, 9).

These words are spoken about the disciples. But Jesus also prays for believers today:

> "My prayer is not for them alone. I pray also for those who will believe in me through their message, that all of them may be one, Father, just as you are in me and I am in you. May they also be in us so that the world may believe that you have sent me" (John 17:20-21).

What an amazing thing to be included among those out of the world for whom Jesus died and for whom he continues to pray!

In his first epistle the apostle John writes to "you who believe in the name of the Son of God so that you may know that you have eternal life" (5:13). Addressing believers, John gives insight into how it happened:

> This is how God showed his love among us: He sent his one and only Son into the world that we might live through him. This is love: not that we loved God, but that he loved us and sent his Son as an atoning sacrifice for our sins (1 John 4:9-10).

For whom did Jesus die? For whom did he make atonement on the cross? Some people think that Jesus died for all people, but that his intention is frustrated by people who do not believe. Could the purpose of the Almighty God ever be frustrated by mere humans? No. It is true that the sacrifice of Jesus is sufficient for the sins of the whole world, but the sacrifice is effectively applied only to those whom God has chosen. Some people think that Jesus set out to save everyone, but that people can reject that offered salvation. If so, Jesus did not accomplish the atonement he wanted to accomplish, for Jesus himself said, "I have brought you (the Father) glory on earth by completing the work you gave me to do" (John 17:4).

The atonement was *accomplished* by Jesus on the cross. He said, "It is finished" (John 19:30). The atonement is *applied* by the Holy Spirit. Jesus said, "No one can come to me unless the Father who sent me draws him" (John 6:44). It is the work of the Holy Spirit to draw believers to Christ.

Questions

1. When children say, "I didn't do it on purpose," they sometimes mean, "It was an accident." What else might they mean?

2. Jesus was intentional about offering himself as a sacrifice on the cross (Luke 18:31-33). What was his purpose in dying on the cross?

3. What is the difference between reconciliation and atonement? (You may want to check with a Bible dictionary.) Which comes first?

4. Jesus once said: "I am the way and the truth and the life. No one comes to the Father except through me" (John 14:6). Why is Jesus the only possible way to God? Why is Jesus the only possible sacrifice for sin?

5. Can God's plans or intentions ever be thwarted by human effort? Why?

6. The Bible says that Jesus came to "save his people from their sins" (Matt. 1:21). To whom does "his people" refer? Does "his people" include you?

Chapter 4

Transformed by the Holy Spirit

"F" is for Fallen Humankind

"A" is for Adopted by God

"I" is for Intentional Atonement

"T" is for Transformed by the Holy Spirit

"H" is for Held by God

"T" stands for "transformed by the Holy Spirit." Once the atonement has been made, how is it to be applied to believers? By the work of the Holy Spirit. The Holy Spirit enables believers to understand spiritual things and begin to live in harmony with God.

The apostle Paul touches on this point:

> Those who are unspiritual do not receive the gifts of God's Spirit, for they are foolishness to them, and they are unable to understand them because they are spiritually discerned (1 Cor. 2:14, NRSV).

Paul teaches that the Holy Spirit works in our hearts: "God has poured out his love into our hearts by the Holy Spirit, whom he has given us" (Rom. 5:5).

The Holy Spirit replaces our rebellious, stony hearts with warm, receptive hearts (Ezek. 36:26). The Holy Spirit opens our hearts to receive the things of God (Acts 16:14), gives us the gift of faith (Eph. 2:8-10), and removes our spiritual blindness (John 9:35-41). The Holy Spirit does all of these things to apply the atonement to our lives.

The idea that the atonement is merely accomplished by Christ but is applied by human beings is not true. It is also not true that Jesus only purchased our redemption on the cross while we supply the faith, so that we work together with Jesus to accomplish our salvation. Becoming a believer is not a cooperative effort. Regeneration (being "born again") is not a result of placing our faith in Jesus; rather, it precedes faith. We are "born anew" by the Holy Spirit, and only then are we able to believe! Salvation is entirely God's gracious work.

In his book *Grace Unknown*, R. C. Sproul says that God did not merely provide potential salvation (offering salvation through the atoning work of Jesus) but actual salvation (because the Holy Spirit empowers us to believe).

> The issue is this: Was God's purpose to make salvation for all possible, or to make salvation for the elect certain? The ultimate aim of God's plan of redemption was to redeem his elect. To accomplish this end he ordained the means. One was the atonement made by his Son. Another was the Holy Spirit's application of this atonement to the elect. God provides for his elect all that is necessary for their salvation, including the gift of faith.
>
> Once we grasp the doctrine of total depravity (humanity's total fall), we know that human beings will not incline themselves to faith in the atoning work of Christ. If God does not supply the means of appropriating the atonement's benefits, namely faith, then the potential redemption of all would result in the actual redemption of none (p. 174). . . .
>
> What the unregenerate person desperately needs in order to come to faith is regeneration. This is the necessary grace. It is the *sine qua non* of salvation. Unless God changes the disposition of my sinful heart, I will never choose to cooperate with grace or embrace Christ in faith. . . . Saving grace does not *offer* liberation, it liberates. Saving grace does not merely offer regeneration, it regenerates. This is what makes grace so gracious: God . . . does for us what we cannot do for ourselves (p. 188).

While we are talking about this work of the Holy Spirit, I would like to take a short excursion into church history to demonstrate that the matter we are dealing with is not new.

In the fifth century A.D. a man named Pelagius began teaching that humankind was born good (that is, without a sinful nature and not prone to sin). He taught that human beings had not fallen into sin and, therefore, had the ability to choose either good or evil. As a result, there was no need for the transforming work of the Holy Spirit to change hearts.

This teaching, which became known as Pelagianism, was studied in the light of the Bible and rejected by the church at the Synod of Carthage in A.D. 418, again at the Council of Ephesus in A.D. 431, and again at the Synod of Orange in A.D. 529.

Eleven centuries later, in the sixteenth century A.D., Pelagianism reappeared through the teachings of a Dutch theologian named Arminius and his followers. Known as Arminianism, it was also dubbed semi-Pelagianism because it taught that humankind has partially fallen rather than not fallen at all. It also taught that people only have *some* good qualities, rather than being completely good. The end result, however, is the same for both Pelagianism and semi-Pelagianism. Both maintain that people are still able to choose Christ without the help of the Holy Spirit. Salvation becomes a cooperative effort— God redeems and humanity believes.

This teaching was found to be contrary to Scripture and rejected at the Synod of Dort in A.D. 1618-1619. The statements of this synod, called the Canons of Dort, are summarized by the acronym F.A.I.T.H.

Questions

1. When a fat green caterpillar turns into a graceful monarch butterfly, we exclaim, "What a transformation!" How does the transforming work of the Holy Spirit differ from the transformations we see in nature?

2. Why is transformation by the Holy Spirit necessary?

3. Although we don't know exactly how the Holy Spirit transforms people, we can see the effects. What are some effects of the transforming work of the Holy Spirit in people's lives?

4. Do you need to be transformed?

Chapter 5

Held by God

"F" is for Fallen Humankind

"A" is for Adopted by God

"I" is for Intentional Atonement

"T" is for Transformed by the Holy Spirit

"H" is for Held by God

"H" stands for "held by God." We are held by God securely for all eternity. This is the joyous conclusion of the matter.

People express the notion of being held by God in different ways:

- "Once saved, always saved": We cannot lose our salvation.

- "Perseverance of the saints": Saints are sinners saved by grace. We persevere through to the end, through to heaven.

- "The perseverance of God": It is really God who perseveres, not us. God brings us through.

- "The preservation of the saints": Again, the emphasis is on God's action, not ours.

- "Eternal security": Our destiny is certain.

What does understanding the doctrines of grace mean to me? It means I do not have to worry about losing my salvation. I am held by God.

Listen to the teaching of Scripture:

> In him you also, who have heard the word of truth, the gospel
> of your salvation, and have believed in him, were sealed with
> the promised Holy Spirit, which is the guarantee of our inher-
> itance until we acquire possession of it, to the praise of his
> glory (Eph. 1:13-14, RSV).

We have an inheritance in heaven, but right now we have the guarantee that
we will indeed receive it. That guarantee is the presence of the Holy Spirit within us. With that guarantee in hand (or should I say "in heart"!), we do not have
to worry that we might lose heaven in the very end.

> Praise be to the God and Father of our Lord Jesus Christ! In his
> great mercy he has given us new birth into a living hope
> through the resurrection of Jesus Christ from the dead, and into
> an inheritance that can never perish, spoil or fade—kept in
> heaven for you, who through faith are shielded by God's power
> until the coming of the salvation that is ready to be revealed in
> the last time (1 Pet. 1:3-5).

We have an eternal inheritance. And God is protecting it for us.

In John's gospel, the Jewish leaders gathered around Jesus and asked him,
"How long will you keep us in suspense? If you are the Christ, tell us plainly."

> Jesus answered, "I did tell you, but you do not believe. The
> miracles I do in my Father's name speak for me, but you do not
> believe because you are not my sheep. My sheep listen to my
> voice; I know them, and they follow me. I give them eternal
> life, and they shall never perish; no one can snatch them out of
> my hand. My Father, who has given them to me, is greater than
> all; no one can snatch them out of my Father's hand. I and the
> Father are one" (John 10:24-30).

There is the image right in Scripture—held by God. A popular insurance
advertisement claims, "You're in good hands with Allstate." The Bible tells us
that we are in better hands with God. No one, not even Satan himself, can
snatch us out of God's hands.

The apostle Paul's letter to the Roman church begins by explaining that all
people—both Jews and Gentiles—are sinners in need of salvation, "for all
have sinned and fall short of the glory of God" (Rom. 3:23). It goes on to reveal
that people are saved through faith in Jesus—"the wages of sin is death, but the

gift of God is eternal life in Christ Jesus our Lord" (Rom. 6:23)—and that the grateful response of those who are saved is a life of service (sin–salvation–service). Romans 8:29-30 explains how "those God foreknew he also predestined. . . . And those he predestined, he also called; those he called, he also justified; those he justified, he also glorified." Then Paul raises the question of our eternal security.

> Who shall separate us from the love of Christ? Shall trouble or hardship or persecution or famine or nakedness or danger or sword? As it is written: "For your sake we face death all day long; we are considered as sheep to be slaughtered." No, in all these things we are more than conquerors through him who loved us. For I am convinced that neither death nor life, neither angels nor demons, neither the present nor the future, nor any powers, neither height nor depth, nor anything else in all creation, will be able to separate us from the love of God that is in Christ Jesus our Lord (Rom. 8:35-39).

What a fantastic statement! Nothing in all of heaven or earth can separate us from the love of God. Why? Because our salvation does not depend on us. It depends totally on God. Many Christians today do not experience the peace and joy that Jesus Christ brings because they are afraid that they can lose their salvation. They think that their salvation depends on their faith; they're afraid that a lapse in their faith will cause them to fall out of God's hand.

In contrast, the Bible teaches that our eternal security does not depend on our hanging on to God, but on God holding on to us. Picture a father and his son holding hands, walking along a treacherous path. If the child is holding onto his father's hand and lets go, he can fall. If the father is holding securely onto the child's hand, the child is safe. The comfort of Scripture is not that believers are hanging on to God, but that God is holding on to them. Salvation is completely God's work. We can rest secure in God's loving grip.

Questions

1. Tell about your earliest memory of being held by the strong, protective hands (or arms) of a loving adult. How did you feel?

2. The Bible teaches that believers are held by God. How does that truth make you feel? How does it affect your behavior?

3. The Bible also teaches that God's grip on believers is stronger than our grip on God. Why might this be a source of comfort for believers?

4. Can such assurance of salvation make a believer careless about Christian living? Why?

5. How might you combat any tendencies toward careless living?

Chapter 6

Another Way of Saying It

We have learned the doctrines of grace using the acronym F.A.I.T.H.:

- **Fallen Humankind.** People, by nature, are dead in sin and therefore completely unable to save themselves from sin and its consequences.

- **Adopted by God.** In love, God has chosen some people to be members of his family.

- **Intentional Atonement.** Jesus died to save his people from their sins.

- **Transformed by the Holy Spirit.** The Spirit regenerates those who are chosen by God, giving them faith in Jesus.

- **Held by God.** Believers are held safe in God's hands for all eternity.

For centuries a different acronym—T.U.L.I.P.—has been used to teach these truths. I have introduced the F.A.I.T.H. acronym because T.U.L.I.P. is often misunderstood. A learning aid that no longer clarifies is best updated.

Nevertheless, since T.U.L.I.P. is so well-known, we should become acquainted with this "other way of saying it."

Total Depravity

"T" is for Total Depravity
"U" is for Unconditional Election
"L" is for Limited Atonement
"I" is for Irresistible Grace
"P" is for Perseverance of the Saints

"T" stands for "total depravity," a phrase that describes the condition of fallen humankind. It speaks of humanity's sin. But when they hear the phrase "total depravity," some people mistakenly think the Bible teaches that people are as bad as they possibly can be—utterly depraved. That is not correct. Instead it means that people are so completely affected by their sinful nature that they are totally unable to contribute anything to their own salvation.

Unconditional Election

"T" is for Total Depravity
"U" is for Unconditional Election
"L" is for Limited Atonement
"I" is for Irresistible Grace
"P" is for Perseverance of the Saints

"U" stands for "unconditional election," which means that God chose certain people before the world was created to be adopted into his family. Unconditional election does not mean that no conditions needed to be met for persons to be chosen by God. Certainly Jesus had to meet all the conditions of the law. He had to fulfill all righteousness in order to bring believers into the presence of the holy God.

The phrase "unconditional election" distinguishes this doctrine from the teaching that election is a *conditional* act by God, that if people meet certain conditions, God will choose them.

What does it mean to meet conditions? Some years back I traded my old Ford LTD for a newer Oldsmobile. I placed some conditions on the sale because I wanted to make sure that the Olds could pull my trailer. I said to the salesman, "I will buy that car *if* you take the heavy-duty hitch off my LTD and put it on the Olds, *if* you take the extra radiator cooler from the Ford and put it on the Olds, *if* you do this and *if* you do that." If he met those conditions, then I would purchase the car. That is the sense of conditional election. It would be as if God were to tell us, "You have to meet certain conditions before I will choose you to be one of my children."

We understand God's election to be unconditional. God did not say: "I will let you be one of my children *if* you are a very good person, or *if* you are attractive, or *if* you earn a minimum of $40,000 per year, or *if* you have faith." And that's a good thing because there is no person on earth who could meet God's conditions.

Where did the idea of conditional election come from? It comes from a misunderstanding of Romans 8:29-30:

> For those God foreknew he also predestined to be conformed to the likeness of his Son, that he might be the firstborn among many brothers. And those he predestined, he also called; those he called, he also justified; those he justified, he also glorified.

Those who favor conditional election understand God's foreknowledge to mean that God knows who would have faith throughout history, and then chooses them because of their faith. These people met the condition of having faith. However, the word "know" in the Bible is often used in the sense of knowing intimately—that is, loving. Genesis 4 tells us that Adam *knew* his wife Eve, and she became pregnant. He loved her in an intimate sense. Similarly, those whom God *foreloved* God predestined. Our election comes simply from God's love and mercy, not by way of our meeting the condition of faith.

> Now, if we are not really ashamed of the Gospel, we must of necessity acknowledge . . . that God by His eternal goodwill (for which there was no other cause than His own purpose), appointed those whom he pleased unto salvation, rejecting all the rest; and that those whom He blessed with this free adoption to be His sons He illumines by His Holy Spirit, that they may receive the life which is offered to them in Christ; while others, continuing of their own will in unbelief, are left destitute of the light of faith, in total darkness.

—John Calvin, "A Treatise on the Eternal Predestination of God," trans. Henry Cole in *Calvin's Calvinism*, p. 31, © 1987, a reprint by Reformed Free Publishing Association, Grand Rapids, Michigan.

Limited Atonement

"T" is for Total Depravity
"U" is for Unconditional Election
"L" is for Limited Atonement
"I" is for Irresistible Grace
"P" is for Perseverance of the Saints

"L" stands for "limited atonement." Here, again, the phrase may fail to communicate accurately the teaching of Scripture. Some people understand "limited atonement" to mean that the sacrifice of Jesus is limited in its power, that it is not sufficient to cover the sins of the whole world. In truth, the blood shed by Jesus on the cross *is* sufficient to cover the sins of the world. The Bible plainly teaches that anyone who believes in Jesus will be saved. His sacrifice accomplished its purpose. The limitation of the atonement is in its application. It is limited to those who are chosen by God. Thus, some people prefer the term "particular atonement" or "purposeful atonement." The atonement is big enough, is sufficient to cover the sins of the world, but it is applied only to those who are born of the Spirit. In other words, it is *sufficient* to cover the sin of all, but *efficient* (effective) only for the elect. It is an intentional atonement.

Irresistible Grace

"T" is for Total Depravity
"U" is for Unconditional Election
"L" is for Limited Atonement
"I" is for Irresistible Grace
"P" is for Perseverance of the Saints

"I" stands for "irresistible grace." Does God drag people into heaven against their will? Some people characterize irresistible grace in this way. The truth is that God does not work against our will, rather God loves us and draws us to himself. The Holy Spirit regenerates us so that we desire God and God's will.

Many people have experienced this truth in their lives. They fought God, but God kept after them until they finally said yes. One of the prime examples of this work of the Spirit is British author and professor C. S. Lewis. He kept holding God off, until finally one night he could resist no longer. In his book *Surprised by Joy* Lewis writes that he "knelt and prayed: perhaps that night, the most dejected and reluctant convert in all England." It was not a big, emotional thing; it was simply irresistible. Lewis later used a phrase from the poet

T. S. Eliot describing God as the "hound of heaven." God going after his people is like a hound on the trail of a fox. God kept pursuing Lewis until God caught him. Lewis said, "I was never so happy as to be caught."

R. C. Sproul writes, "Regeneration is a supernatural work . . . of recreation by which the dead are raised and brought to . . . a living faith, through which they are saved and adopted into the family of God" (*Grace Unknown,* p. 196).

Perseverance of the Saints

"T" is for Total Depravity
"U" is for Unconditional Election
"L" is for Limited Atonement
"I" is for Irresistible Grace
"P" is for Perseverance of the Saints

"P" stands for "perseverance of the saints." Perhaps it would be more accurate to speak of the *preservation* of God. Believers persevere in their faith because God preserves his own people. We are held by God, and therefore are assured of our salvation.

Questions

1. Share an acronym, poem, saying, or proverb that helps you remember something. (For example, "Lefty loosy/righty tighty" helps some people remember which way to turn a bottle cap.)

2. Two acronyms (F.A.I.T.H. and T.U.L.I.P.) have been introduced as tools to help you remember the doctrines of grace. Which do you find most helpful? Why?

3. Someone once said of these teachings: "These doctrines are not hard to understand; but they are difficult to accept." Do you agree? Why or why not?

Questions and Answers

Learning about the doctrines of grace raises questions for some people. Here are some common questions and answers.

1. Must a person be elected (chosen) in order to be saved?

Ultimately the answer is yes. A person who is not elect cannot come to faith in God because it is only the Holy Spirit who gives faith. The Bible says that we are "dead in our trespasses and sins." We are unable to believe unless the Holy Spirit transforms us. This is seen more clearly after the fact, after coming to believe in Jesus. Following your rebirth, you might look back and say, "Wow! This is even more magnificent than I realized. God not only provided atonement on the cross, but he also implanted saving faith in my heart that enabled me to believe!"

Imagine an old, rural cemetery with brick pillars on either side of the entrance and metalwork arching over the top. Picture that as the gate of heaven. As you walk up to the gate you read the words on the iron arch:

Whosoever Will May Come. You walk through the gate, turn around, and read what it says on the back: Chosen From All Eternity. Many people think, when they first put their faith in Jesus, that trusting him is a step they took on their own. Only afterward, looking deeper into the teaching of the Bible, do they realize that it was the Holy Spirit who enabled them to believe. Then it becomes clear that *all* the praise and *all* the glory go to God.

2. But isn't it unfair of God to choose only some and not all?

While I was teaching a group of students as a campus pastor, a young woman in the front row raised her hand and said to me, "It's not fair that God chose some and passed by others." I invited her to look at Romans 9, where the apostle Paul uses the story of Jacob and Esau to illustrate the fact that God chose the Israelites out of all the peoples of the world:

> Just as it is written: "Jacob I loved, but Esau I hated." What then shall we say? Is God unjust? Not at all! For he says to Moses, "I will have mercy on whom I have mercy, and I will have compassion on whom I have compassion." It does not, therefore, depend on man's desire or effort, but on God's mercy (vv. 13-16).

What is the basis of election? It has nothing to do with an individual's will, exertion, or actions. It is based entirely on God's mercy. Paul continues with another example from the Old Testament, from the time of the exodus of the Israelites from Egypt:

> For the Scripture says to Pharaoh: "I raised you up for this very purpose, that I might display my power in you and that my name might be proclaimed in all the earth. Therefore God has mercy on whom he wants to have mercy, and he hardens whom he wants to harden" (Rom. 9:17-18).

This picture of God may seem foreign to us. Have you ever thought of God hardening somebody's heart so that they would not obey God? That is what the Bible teaches. How are we to understand this? Review the account of Pharaoh and the ten plagues God sent on the Egyptian nation in Exodus 7-11. In response to Pharaoh's persistent refusal to allow the Israelites to leave Egypt, God sent devastating plagues. After the first three plagues, Scripture says that Pharaoh hardened his heart and refused to allow the Israelites to leave. But after the fourth plague there is a subtle change in the way the result is reported: "And God hardened Pharaoh's heart."

There comes a point where God gives us what we want. Pharaoh continually hardened his heart until he reached the point where God said, "OK, Pharaoh, so be it." That is a very sobering message. Many people think they can reject God throughout their entire lives and then have a deathbed conversion. The Bible teaches that there is a point of no return. "Today is the day of salvation." Believe now! It is possible that God will give you what you want instead of what you need.

So yes, God hardened Pharaoh's heart. But it wasn't as if Pharaoh wanted to believe and God wouldn't let him. Pharaoh continually persisted in unbelief and received his just reward. We too are worthy only of condemnation. Only because of God's gracious choice are we adopted into his family.

3. If it is God who selects the saved, then why blame us for unbelief?

The questioning college student continued: "Well, if it is God who can open the heart and God who hardens the heart, then why does God find fault with us? We really don't have any say about it. Why blame us?" I suggested we look further at Romans 9.

> One of you will say to me: "Then why does God still blame us? For who resists his will?" But who are you, O man, to talk back to God? "Shall what is formed say to him who formed it, 'Why did you make me like this?'" Does not the potter have the right to make out of the same lump of clay some pottery for noble purposes and some for common use? What if God, choosing to show his wrath and make his power known, bore with great patience the objects of his wrath—prepared for destruction? What if he did this to make the riches of his glory known to the objects of his mercy, whom he prepared in advance for glory— even us, whom he also called, not only from the Jews but also from the Gentiles (vv. 19-24)?

Did Paul answer the question? Not quite. The question is, "Why does God still judge or find fault with us if it is God who chooses for adoption?" Paul replies, "Good question. But your questions have gone far enough. Who are you, a mere human being, to question God? Doesn't a potter have the right to fashion clay into the vessel of his own choosing? Doesn't God have the same right? Isn't God the one who is in charge?"

In a sense, Paul does not answer the question. He simply replies, "Your questions have gone far enough." We know this much, but we don't know everything. To know everything would mean that we are God, and we are not. There is a clear distinction between God and God's creation.

We are now approaching that line, and we cannot go over it without claiming to be God. We are God's creation. God's thoughts are beyond our thoughts. We must remain content with the information he has revealed and leave the rest in the realm of mystery, all the while remembering that God is both merciful and just.

> It is important to remember that in his decree of election, God considers the mass of mankind in their fallen sinful condition. He chooses to redeem some people from this condition and to leave the rest in that condition. He intervenes in the lives of the elect, while he does not intervene in the lives of the reprobate. One group receives mercy and the other receives justice.
>
> —R. C. Sproul, *Grace Unknown*, p. 160

4. Is it possible for one of God's chosen sons or daughters never to repent and believe?

No, that is not possible. Repenting and believing are the results of being "transformed by the Spirit." Because God the Holy Spirit regenerates us, we are given new life. And having been given new life, we will believe. The apostle Paul writes:

> At one time we too were foolish, disobedient, deceived and enslaved by all kinds of passions and pleasures. We lived in malice and envy, being hated and hating one another. But when the kindness and love of God our Savior appeared, he saved us, not because of righteous things we had done, but because of his mercy. He saved us through the washing of rebirth and renewal by the Holy Spirit, whom he poured out on us generously through Jesus Christ our Savior, so that, having been justified by his grace, we might become heirs having the hope of eternal life (Titus 3:3-7).

It is the work of God within us as well as the work of God on the cross that assures us that we will come to salvation.

It is possible, however, to abuse this teaching of Scripture. One might say: "Well, if I am one of God's elect I will be saved no matter what, so I will just live it up. God will save me just before I die." But you are not really thinking God's thoughts if you reason this way, are you? The correct response to God's merciful adoption is to live in thankfulness and gratitude as his children. Paul continues this thought in Titus 3:8:

> This is a trustworthy saying. And I want you to stress these things, so that those who have trusted in God may be careful to devote themselves to doing what is good. These things are excellent and profitable for everyone.

5. Could it be true, though, that a person could go halfway (or more) through life before accepting Christ?

Yes, it is possible. One of the greatest theologians and a teacher of these doctrines was St. Augustine. His mother prayed for him for years while he lived a life filled with sin. He was midway through life before his mother's prayers were answered and he became a Christian. Augustine was "born anew," and he personally experienced God's merciful adoption. He experienced salvation and then understood how God had worked in his life.

Our evangelistic efforts should seldom begin with teaching the doctrine of election. When talking with people who are not believers, do not start by saying, "You know the Bible teaches that either you are elect or you are not." This may lead them to draw wrong conclusions. We should begin with prayer, for it is the Holy Spirit who changes hearts. We should begin with humankind's fallen condition and need of salvation. We should point out God's provision in Jesus Christ. We should call them to respond. "Believe in the Lord Jesus, and you will be saved" (Acts 16:31). Once they respond, we can point out how the Holy Spirit worked within them so they were *able* to respond. Then their understanding and joy and gratitude to God will be all the deeper. And they will live for him.

6. What about people who at one time claimed to be Christians but now have nothing to do with Christ or his church? At one time they seemed to be Christians, but now they seem to have fallen away.

There are two possibilities concerning the condition of such people. One is that they are backsliding spiritually. Think of children pulling sleds up a snowy hill. They make their way to the top, but not without slipping back a bit from time to time. Some Christians experience life like that. They believe, but they have lapses in their Christian lives. They slide backwards occasionally, but they ever keep moving forward in Christ. They live for God. Since God has his hand on them, they ultimately will remain faithful.

The second possibility is that they were never saved in the first place. They had all the external Christian characteristics. They did the things Christians do: they came to worship; they sang the songs; they lived good moral lives. But their hearts had never been changed. Their "Christianity" is superficial. It is difficult to assess their true spiritual state because only God can look on the heart. Only God knows who has truly been converted.

Our response in either case is the same. The individual must be brought face-to-face with the demands of God's Word. We might challenge those who are backsliding to consider their relationship to Jesus and to reflect on the inappropriate choices they are making. They can then repent of their sin and determine to live in a renewed way. On the other hand, if we are talking to those who have some Christian characteristics but have never been converted, our question about their relationship to Jesus becomes a call to salvation. It is not necessary for us to know whether the person is a backslider or unbeliever. In either case, the solution is to call them to a walk with the Lord.

7. Won't belief in being "held by God" cause some to live sinful lives since they know they will somehow be saved anyhow?

"Let's eat, drink, and be merry, for tomorrow we're saved." "Paint the town brown, your salvation is secured." "Once saved, it doesn't matter how you live." "Now that I know I am one of God's chosen people and that I am held securely in his hand and cannot lose my salvation, I am free to live a life of sin." These misrepresentations of the doctrines of grace are not new. Paul met them head-on in Romans 6:1-2:

> What shall we say, then? Shall we go on sinning so that grace
> may increase? By no means! We died to sin; how can we live in
> it any longer?

Once we have been regenerated, we are changed for life! Listen to what Jesus says:

> I am the vine, you are the branches. Those who abide in me
> and I in them bear much fruit, because apart from me you can
> do nothing (John 15:5, NRSV).

So if you are in Christ, if you have been grafted into the vine, the necessary result is producing fruit (good deeds). You will live a Christian life. It is natural if the graft has taken. If someone says, "I am in the vine," but is producing bad fruit or no fruit at all, you may need to check the graft by asking, "Are you really in the vine?" "Are you really in Christ?" "What is your relationship to Jesus Christ?"

Those who are truly "in Christ" will reject the notion that they can sin more and without consequence, because that simply does not happen. The apostle John makes this very clear:

> If we claim to have fellowship with him yet walk in the darkness, we lie and do not live by the truth (1 John 1:6).

> The man who says, "I know him," but does not do what he commands is a liar, and the truth is not in him (1 John 2:4).

> No one who is born of God will continue to sin, because God's seed remains in him; he cannot go on sinning, because he has been born of God. This is how we know who the children of God are and who the children of the devil are: Anyone who does not do what is right is not a child of God; nor is anyone who does not love his brother (1 John 3:9-10).

If we really understand the seriousness of our condition prior to Christ—that we were dead in our trespasses and sins and that through the grace of God we are born again—we will respond with a life of good, not evil. The notion that grace gives us license to sin more turns grace on its head. The very idea is impossible. The only right response to God's grace is thanksgiving.

8. Why would missionaries bother to go overseas to preach the gospel if everything is predestined anyway?

God's method for reaching the lost is through the preaching of the gospel:

> "Everyone who calls on the name of the Lord will be saved." How, then, can they call on the one they have not believed in? And how can they believe in the one of whom they have never heard? And how can they hear without someone preaching to them? And how can they preach unless they are sent? As it is written, "How beautiful are the feet of those who bring good news!" (Rom. 10:13-15).

God calls believers to go into all the world and make disciples of all nations and baptize them in the name of the Father, Son, and Holy Spirit (Matt. 28:19-20). God has given us that mission. God has made us his partners in gathering his elect into the church of Jesus Christ. He did not have to do that. Jesus said to the people who were not giving him proper recognition as the Messiah, "I could have these stones cry out." There are other ways God could have gotten the word out. But he chose to include us in his mission to the world!

In fact, understanding these doctrines of grace helps us in our outreach. Think back to the Bible's teaching about fallen humankind (the "F" in our acronym). People by nature are dead in their trespasses and sins. They cannot even hear the gospel. Can you think of anything more frustrating than trying to communicate the gospel or preaching to someone who is dead? What a fruitless task! Some years ago I had a bout with laryngitis. I was not able to preach on Sunday morning. That really sent the elders of the church scrambling! They later asked me to record one of my sermons so they could play the tape over the sound system if that ever happened again. So I did. I went into my office, got out my sermon, set the tape recorder to record, and literally preached to a brick wall! That was really hard to do because there was no response—no people listening, no facial expressions to tell me that they were understanding. I was preaching to a brick wall. And that is what *all* preaching would be were it not for the doctrines of grace.

When we go out with the gospel, however, we can go with confidence because we know God's chosen people will respond positively. God's elect will respond in faith. They will come to him in response to the gospel and be drawn into his church. Without this teaching of Scripture, the whole notion of missions and evangelizing the world would be impossible—it would be like preaching to a brick wall. The doctrines of grace are an encouragement—not a discouragement—for the missionary enterprise of the church. When missionaries go to other lands, they can be confident that God's chosen ones are there too, and that those people will respond to the gospel. The Bible reminds us that in heaven there are people from every tribe, every tongue, and every nation of the world (Rev. 5:9).

Questions

Discussion questions for chapters 7 and 8 appear at the end of chapter 8.

The Great Mystery

The relationship between God's sovereignty and human responsibility is a great mystery. Even with all the preceding explanation, the revealed truth is difficult to grasp; it is beyond our ability to understand completely.

By "God's sovereignty" we mean that God rules all things; God controls all things; God is in charge of all things. God's will *will* be done. By "human responsibility" we mean that people have a will of their own. We are responsible beings—responsible to believe, responsible to repent of our sin, and responsible to confess Jesus as our Savior and Lord. The Bible teaches both of these truths. In speaking of God's sovereignty, it emphasizes the activity of God in salvation (loving, choosing, calling, regenerating, and the like). In speaking of human responsibility, it emphasizes the activity of individuals in salvation (repenting, confessing, believing, following, and the like). These two truths may seem to be in tension, even contradictory. Yet the Bible teaches them both.

When one is emphasized at the expense of the other, we run into difficulty. For example, the Arminian understanding of the Bible tends to overemphasize human responsibility. Simply stated, Arminians teach that God has provided the way of salvation, but people must provide faith. Salvation becomes a cooperative effort—God provides the atonement through the death and resurrection of his Son Jesus; people provide the necessary faith in order to receive Christ's sacrifice. Put the two together and salvation is the result. The problem with this teaching is that God ends up as less than sovereign.

As we have seen, the Bible teaches that before the world was created God chose some people to adopt into his spiritual family and that the chosen will indeed come to full and final salvation. Arminianism, however, teaches that a person can resist God's choosing. For example, let's say that we need to pick teams for a softball game. I am one of the captains and I choose you to be on my team. But you say, "I don't want to be on your team." You refuse my selection of you. Although I want you to play on my team, I am powerless to make it happen. Now apply that to God's selection of you. If you can resist God's choosing, you end up with a God who is not all-powerful. God is not almighty if you can overrule his decrees. The Arminian view cannot be correct.

On the other hand, some people overemphasize the sovereignty of God. This is called hyper- or ultra-Calvinism. Undue stress on the idea that God does what God wants to do strips individuals of their will and responsibility. They become like robots with no will of their own. They merely do as they are told. A human without a will is no longer human. The Bible teaches that people do have a will. (The problem, you will recall, is that because of sin they choose the wrong. That is why God provides a rebirth, enabling them to choose the right.)

So the Bible teaches both that God is sovereign and that humans are responsible beings. How can we understand this? Here is an illustration. When I was a teenager I loved working with horses. Daily I would go to a dude ranch and work—most of the time shoveling "processed oats" in the barn. Above the ground floor of that barn was a trap door leading into the hayloft, and coming out of the trap door were two ropes. Applying basic geometry, those ropes looked like two parallel lines reaching off into infinity. It looked like they would never meet.

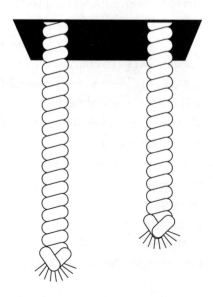

But when you climbed a ladder into the hayloft you discovered that from the central beam of the barn hung a large pulley, and what had looked like two ropes had all the time been one rope looped over that pulley.

That is the difficulty we face when we try to resolve with our finite minds and from our earthly perspective the mystery of God's sovereignty and human responsibility. We do not have the heavenly perspective. Our vision is cut short. When we get to heaven and understand things from the heavenly perspective, we will see that there is really no contradiction at all. In the meantime, we simply have to believe both in God's sovereignty and in human responsibility, hold both in tension, and not lose either one. For, if we lose one or the other, we end up with a God who is too small or a human who is no human at all.

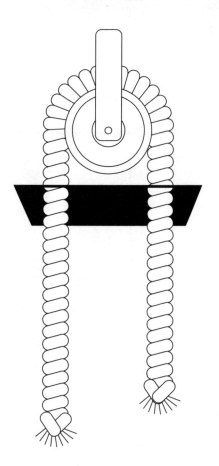

Questions

These discussion questions cover chapters 7 and 8.

1. In chapters 7 and 8 the author answers common questions about these teachings. Which question was on your mind? Did the author's answer help you? Do you have a question that was not addressed? What is it?

2. Do you think we will ever fully understand God's purposes in this life? Why?

3. Why is it difficult to live with unresolved questions? What is the place of faith in doing so?

4. Why is it important to believe in both God's sovereignty and human responsibility?

Why Did God Reveal This?

In a sense we do not need to know all that God has revealed to us in the doctrines of grace. We might say this is "behind the scenes" material. All we really need are these words from Scripture: "Believe on the Lord Jesus Christ and you will be saved." So why did God reveal to us just how desperate our need is—that we are completely fallen and unable to contribute anything to our salvation? Why did God reveal that he chose to adopt us into his family from before the creation of the world? Why did God reveal to us that Jesus came to "save his people from their sins"? Why the revelation that even our believing is dependent on God's grace—that transformation by the Holy Spirit enables us to believe? Why do we need to know that God holds us for all eternity? How will such knowledge benefit us? There are many reasons, I suppose, but let me list some of them.

1. **It reveals the depth of God's great love for us.** The Bible sings of this theme:

> But God demonstrates his own love for us in this: while we were still sinners, Christ died for us (Rom. 5:8).

> For he chose us in him before the creation of the world to be holy and blameless in his sight. In love he predestined us to be adopted as his sons through Jesus Christ, in accordance with his pleasure and will (Eph. 1:4-5).

> But because of his great love for us, God, who is rich in mercy, made us alive with Christ even when we were dead in transgressions—it is by grace you have been saved (Eph. 2:4-5).

> For we know, brothers and sisters beloved by God, that he has chosen you, because our message of the gospel came to you not in word only, but also in power and in the Holy Spirit and with full conviction (1 Thess. 1:4-5, NRSV).

> How great is the love the Father has lavished on us, that we should be called children of God (1 John 3:1).

Indeed, knowing the doctrines of grace deepens our knowledge of "how wide and long and high and deep is the love of Christ" (Eph. 3:18).

2. **It reveals the power of love in our lives.** The Bible says that our love is a result of being recipients of God's grace.

> God has poured out his love into our hearts by the Holy Spirit, whom he has given us (Rom. 5:5).

> Dear friends, let us love one another, for love comes from God. Everyone who loves has been born of God and knows God. . . . We love because he first loved us (1 John 4:7, 19).

3. **It reveals the motive for our good works.** That motive is gratitude for what God has done for us.

> "You did not choose me, but I chose you and appointed you to go and bear fruit—fruit that will last" (John 15:16).

4. **It reveals the source of our knowledge.** We do not come to an understanding of the things of God in our own power, nor by human wisdom.

These things God has revealed to us through the Spirit; for the Spirit searches everything, even the depths of God. For what human being knows what is truly human except the human spirit that is within? So also no one comprehends what is truly God's except the Spirit of God. Now we have received not the spirit of the world, but the Spirit that is from God, so that we may understand the gifts bestowed on us by God (1 Cor. 2:10-12, NRSV).

5. **It reveals the nature of our security.** It is eternal, unshakeable.

"I give them eternal life, and they shall never perish; no one can snatch them out of my hand. My Father, who has given them to me is greater than all; no one can snatch them out of my Father's hand. I and the Father are one" (John 10:28-30).

6. **It reveals the depth of our joy.**

Praise be to the God and Father of our Lord Jesus Christ! In his great mercy he has given us new birth into a living hope through the resurrection of Jesus Christ from the dead, and into an inheritance that can never perish, spoil, or fade— kept in heaven for you, who through faith are shielded by God's power until the coming of the salvation that is ready to be revealed in the last time. In this you greatly rejoice, though now for a little while you may have had to suffer grief in all kinds of trials (1 Pet. 1:3-6).

7. **It reveals the breadth of our comfort.**

May your unfailing love be my comfort, according to your promise to your servant (Ps. 119:76).

The Heidelberg Catechism states that my "only comfort in life and in death" is "that I am not my own, but belong—body and soul, in life and in death—to my faithful Savior Jesus Christ. He has fully paid for all my sins with his precious blood, and has set me free from the tyranny of the devil. He also watches over me in such a way that not a hair can fall from my head without the will of my Father in heaven: in fact, all things must work together for my salvation. Because I belong to him, Christ, by his Holy

Spirit, assures me of eternal life and makes me wholeheartedly willing and ready from now on to live for him" (Q&A 1).

8. **It reveals the firmness of our confidence.** Listen to this victory cry from Paul:

> Who will bring any charge against those whom God has chosen? . . .Who shall separate us from the love of Christ? Shall trouble or hardship or persecution or famine or nakedness or danger or sword? . . . No, in all these things we are more than conquerors through him who loved us (Rom. 8:33, 35, 37).

9. **It reveals the cause of our boldness in witness.** We witness with confidence because these doctrines teach us that the results belong to God. Only the Holy Spirit can change a person's heart. So we share the good news, but do not manipulate people. Our witness is a result of God's grace.

> But you are a chosen people, a royal priesthood, a holy nation, a people belonging to God, that you may declare the praises of him who called you out of darkness into his wonderful light (1 Pet. 2:9).

10. **It reveals that we were chosen for a purpose.** God has redeemed us so that we will accomplish his will here on earth. Jesus taught his followers to pray, "Your will be done on earth as it is in heaven" (Matt. 6:10).
    In addition, the apostle Paul reminds us:

> For it is by grace you have been saved, through faith—and this not from yourselves, it is the gift of God—not by works, so that no one can boast. For we are God's workmanship, created in Christ Jesus to do good works, which God prepared in advance for us to do" (Eph. 2:8-10).

11. **It reveals that all the glory goes to God.** Understanding the doctrines of grace moves us away from any temptation to claim a role in our salvation because salvation is totally a work of God. All the glory is his!

> To him who is able to keep you from falling and to present you before his glorious presence without fault and with great joy—to the only God our Savior be glory, majesty, power and

authority, through Jesus Christ our Lord, before all ages, now
and forevermore (Jude 24-25).

So God has revealed these things to us for a purpose. They affect how
we live our Christian life and how we function as a church.

> The secret things belong to the LORD our God; but the things
> that are revealed belong to us and to our children forever,
> that we may do all the words of this law (Deut. 29:29).

These are good words to apply to the doctrines of grace. God has not revealed everything to us. The secret things belong to God and we must trust
him with those. But God has revealed some things, and we are to live by
those. The Christian life is a life of faith. Trusting God even when he has
not revealed everything to us is one side of living by faith. Another side is
living according to what God has revealed. Let us rejoice in the depth and
breadth of the revelation that God has entrusted to us.

Questions

Discussion questions for chapters 9 and 10 appear at the end of chapter 10.

How Do I Know If I Am Elect?

How do I know if I have been chosen and adopted by God? That is the question on the minds of many people who learn of these truths for the first time. How can you be sure that you are among the elect?

A man once said, "There are two ways to know for certain that you are one of God's elect. One is to go to the firehouse and get the world's largest hook-and-ladder truck, extend the ladder up as far as it will go, lean it against the clouds of heaven, climb to the top, peek over the edge, and look into the Book of Life to see if your name is written there. Or you can believe in Jesus Christ as your Savior and Lord."

What did he mean? He was saying that there is actually only one way to know. Obviously you cannot put a ladder against the clouds of heaven and take a peek at the Lamb's Book of Life. The only way you can know is to place your faith in Jesus.

After trusting in Jesus alone for your salvation, you will realize that believing would have been impossible had God not chosen you from all eternity to be adopted into his family. An old hymn puts it this way:

> I sought the Lord, and afterward I knew
> he moved my soul to seek him, seeking me;
> it was not I that found, O Savior true;
> no, I was found, was found of Thee.

Some people wrestle much with the question "How do I know that I am one of God's elect?" The answer is so simple: "Believe in the Lord Jesus Christ and you will be saved" (Acts 16:31).

Questions

These discussion questions cover chapters 9 and 10.

1. Three-year-olds learn the question "Why?" and drive their parents crazy with it. But it's a good question to ask. What is the answer to the title question of chapter 9: "Why did God reveal this?" What are God's reasons for revealing these truths?

2. The author lists eleven reasons why it is helpful for us to know these truths. Do any of these reasons surprise you? Why?

3. Can you think of some other reasons that God revealed the doctrines of grace?

4. Of all the questions in this book, the title question of chapter 10 is most important—"How do I know if I am elect?" What is your answer?

For Further Reading

General

Packer, J. I. *Evangelism and the Sovereignty of God.* Chicago: InterVarsity Press, 1961.

Pink, A. W. *The Sovereignty of God.* London: The Banner of Truth Trust, 1961.

Sproul, R. C. *Grace Unknown.* Grand Rapids, MI: Baker Book House, 1997.

Spurgeon, C. H. *Sermons on Sovereignty.* Ashland, KY: Baptist Examiner Book Shop, 1959.

Chapter 1—Fallen Humankind

Luther, Martin, *The Bondage of the Will,* edited and translated by J. I. Packer and O. R. Johnston. Cambridge: James Clarke/Westwood, NJ: Revell, 1957.

Chapter 2—Adopted by God

Pink, Arthur W. *The Doctrine of Election.* A booklet from Bible Truth Depot.

Sproul, R. C. *Chosen by God.* Wheaton: Tyndale House Publishers, 1986.

Spurgeon, C. H. *Election.* Philadelphia: Great Commission Publications, 1975.

Chapter 3—Intentional Atonement

Kuiper, R. B. *For Whom Did Christ Die?* Grand Rapids, MI: Wm. B. Eerdmans Publishing Co., 1959.

Murray, John. *Redemption—Accomplished and Applied.* Grand Rapids, MI: Wm. B. Eerdmans Publishing Co., 1955.

Chapter 4—Transformed by the Holy Spirit

Palmer, Edwin H. *The Holy Spirit.* Grand Rapids, MI: Baker Book House, 1958.

Sproul, R. C. *The Mystery of the Holy Spirit.* Wheaton: Tyndale House Publishers, 1990.

Chapter 5—Held by God

Sproul, R. C., ed. *Doubt and Assurance.* Grand Rapids, MI: Baker Book House, 1993.